KARMA IS RELATIVE

A Practical Perspective

By:

DR PRATUL SHARMA

Ph.D. IIT DELHI

Written and Compiled with the Help of Artificial Intelligence

FIRST EDITION 2025

All Rights Reserved. No part of this publication can be stored in a retrieval system or reproduced in any form or by any means without the prior written permission of the publishers

LIMITS OF LIABILITY AND DISCLAIMER OF WARRANTY

The Author/Publisher of this book have tried their best to ensure that the contents in the book are correct. The author/publishers make no warranty of any kind, with regard to these contents. The author and publisher shall not be liable for any consequences arising out of the use of this book.

All trademarks referred are acknowledged as properties of their respective owners.

Preface

The concept of karma is one of the most profound and widely discussed ideas in human history. It resonates across cultures, religions, and philosophies, and continues to shape our understanding of life, choices, and consequences. This book, *Karma is Relative*, seeks to explore this ancient principle not only as a spiritual or religious doctrine but as a universal law that governs human existence.

Karma, in its simplest form, suggests that our actions—both good and bad—inevitably shape our future experiences. Yet, its implications stretch far beyond this basic notion. From its roots in Hinduism, Buddhism, and Jainism to its reflections in modern psychology and quantum physics, karma presents a model for understanding the intricacies of human behavior and the interconnectedness of all beings.

The journey through this book begins with an examination of karma's foundational teachings in the scriptures of ancient India, including the Bhagavad Gita, the Upanishads, and the works of great philosophers. We then expand the lens to include perspectives from Buddhism and Jainism, each offering unique insights into the law of cause and effect. The exploration deepens with an inquiry into karma's relevance in contemporary life—how it can influence modern psychology, personal growth, and societal structures.

This book is intended for readers who are curious about the deeper workings of karma and its role in our lives. Whether you are seeking spiritual wisdom, philosophical understanding, or practical guidance for personal transformation, *The Theory of Karma* offers a comprehensive approach to this timeless truth.

Through these pages, I hope to inspire a deeper connection to the actions we take every day and encourage a mindful approach to the life we are creating with every decision.

Contents

Introduction to the Theory of Karma:
A Practical Modern Perspective

1. Definition of Karma

Let's begin with the million-dollar question: What exactly is karma? Is it the cosmic "payback" system? A celestial accountant tallying your deeds? Or just an overused hashtag when your ex gets stuck in traffic on their dream date? Truthfully, karma is far more profound than any pop-culture depiction. At its core, karma is a Sanskrit word meaning "action." Simple, right? But, like all good Sanskrit words, it's deceptively simple. It's not just about the action itself but the intention behind it and the ripple effects it creates.

Think of karma as the universe's cause-and-effect mechanism. What you sow, you reap. If you plant mango seeds, you're not going to grow guavas—unless you live in a particularly mischievous parallel dimension. Every action, whether physical, verbal, or mental, sets off a chain reaction. The effects may not show up immediately (sorry, no instant gratification here), but they're inevitable.

Here's a practical example: Imagine you're at work, and instead of doing your tasks, you spend the day watching cat videos. Funny, sure, but the karma? A last-minute deadline pops up, and you're scrambling to complete your work. The universe might not serve poetic justice every time, but the principle holds: actions have consequences, whether subtle or obvious.

2. Historical and Cultural Significance

Karma has been around longer than your favorite coffee chain, and it's steeped in history and tradition. The concept originates in ancient Indian philosophy, primarily rooted in Hinduism, Buddhism, and Jainism. But don't imagine karma as an old sage sitting cross-legged under a banyan tree; it's more like a universal Wi-Fi network—invisible, always active, and impossible to escape.

The earliest mentions of karma can be found in the Vedas and Upanishads, where it's intertwined with dharma (duty) and moksha (liberation). The Bhagavad Gita, for example, offers a goldmine of wisdom on karma. Krishna tells Arjuna, "Focus on your actions, not the results." Basically, it's ancient

India's way of saying, "Don't obsess over likes and retweets; just do your thing."

Over the centuries, the idea of karma has transcended its spiritual roots. Today, it's a global phenomenon. From self-help books to blockbuster movies, karma has become everyone's favorite universal law. The concept's flexibility—applicable to both grand philosophies and everyday life—makes it timeless.

Take Mahatma Gandhi's life as an example. His belief in nonviolence wasn't just a moral choice but a karmic one. By promoting peace and self-discipline, he set an example for generations. His actions echoed the principle of "good karma" on a monumental scale.

3. Why Understanding Karma Is Relevant Today

Now, let's address the elephant in the room: Why should we care about karma in today's world of algorithms, instant gratification, and fast food? After all, karma doesn't come with a tracking app or a customer support line. Yet, understanding karma is more relevant than ever.

1. The Stress Factor: Modern life is stressful. Deadlines, traffic jams, and those awkward Zoom meetings where you accidentally talk while muted—it's a lot. Karma teaches us to focus on what's in our control: our actions. By letting go of the obsession with results, we can reduce stress. Imagine planting a garden. You can water the plants, give them sunlight, and protect them from pests, but you can't force them to bloom. Understanding karma reminds us to let go of what's beyond our control.

2. Interpersonal Relationships: Ever noticed how being kind to someone—even a stranger—can brighten your day? That's karma in action. It's not about keeping a tally but creating positive energy that flows both ways. For instance, holding the door for someone might seem trivial, but it could inspire a ripple effect of small kindnesses. Now, imagine the opposite—cutting someone off in traffic. Instant karma might not hit you, but you've likely added to their bad day, and the cycle continues.

3. Accountability: In an era of blaming everything on circumstances, karma gently nudges us toward personal accountability. Didn't get that promotion? Before you blame your boss, reflect on your efforts.

Karma isn't about external judgment; it's an internal mirror. The choices you make—big or small—shape your journey.

4. Environmental Responsibility: Think about our collective karma with the environment. Polluting rivers, cutting down forests, and ignoring climate change aren't just poor ecological choices; they're karmic debts. The planet's current state is a direct result of collective human actions. Understanding karma reminds us that our actions today impact the future—for better or worse.

5. Humor in Hardships: Finally, karma offers a philosophical cushion for life's challenges. When life hands you lemons, you can either make lemonade or question if you planted a lemon tree in a past life. Finding humor in karmic lessons can be liberating. For example, if your phone dies just as you're about to make an important call, you can either stress out or laugh at the irony. Maybe it's karma's way of telling you to slow down.

A Practical Wrap-Up

To wrap up, karma isn't just a mystical idea for monks and philosophers. It's a practical guide for modern living. It teaches us to act with intention, take responsibility, and find peace in the process. Life, after all, is like a boomerang. What you throw out into the world—be it kindness, patience, or sarcasm—eventually comes back. So, the next time you're about to send that snarky email, pause and ask yourself, "What kind of boomerang am I throwing?"

Understanding karma helps us live more consciously and harmoniously. It's not about fearing consequences but about creating a life that resonates with positive actions. So, whether you're planting metaphorical mango trees or simply trying to navigate the chaos of daily life, remember: karma's got your back—and your actions are the key to unlocking its magic.

Chapter 1:

Foundational Concepts of Karma

Understanding karma isn't just about knowing the "what" but also diving into the "how" and "why" of this timeless principle. In this chapter, we'll explore the origins of karma, its types, and other related concepts that will help demystify its profound wisdom. Let's take this journey step by step.

---

1. Origin of the Concept of Karma (Vedas and Upanishads)

Karma is not a modern-day concept concocted by life coaches or Instagram influencers. Its roots run deep into ancient Indian scriptures. The earliest mention of karma can be found in the **Vedas**, the oldest texts of Indian spirituality, particularly in the **Rigveda**, which speaks of actions leading to specific outcomes—a precursor to the law of karma. However, the philosophical depth of karma truly unfolds in the **Upanishads**, the concluding portions of the Vedas, which are also called Vedanta.

The Vedic View

In the Vedas, karma initially referred to rituals and sacrifices. It was believed that performing precise actions, like a yajna (fire sacrifice), would invoke the gods' favor and bring prosperity. For example, farmers might conduct a ritual to ensure a bountiful harvest. If the rains came on time, they knew they'd nailed it; if not, perhaps the priest's chant needed work.

The Upanishadic Evolution

The Upanishads, however, shifted the focus from external rituals to inner actions. Here, karma is no longer about appeasing deities but about the individual's journey. The **Brihadaranyaka Upanishad** beautifully states: "A person becomes good by good actions and bad by bad actions." This laid the foundation for understanding karma as a universal law of cause and effect.

Consider this example: If a potter creates a crooked pot, it's not the wheel's fault but the potter's lack of skill. Similarly, our lives are shaped not by fate alone but by our actions and intentions. This profound shift from ritual to responsibility was a game-changer, influencing not just Indian spirituality but global philosophy.

2. Types of Karma: Sanchita, Prarabdha, and Agami/Kriyamana

Think of karma as your cosmic bank account. It's got savings, active balances, and even future deposits. Intriguing, right? Let's break it down:

Sanchita Karma (The Savings Account)

This is the accumulated karma of all your past lives. Every good deed, every mistake—they're all stored here. Think of it as the universe's hard drive that never crashes. However, not all of this karma comes into play in your current life. Imagine you're carrying a suitcase filled with thousands of files, but you're only allowed to open a few during this lifetime.

Example: Let's say you were a generous merchant in a past life, but also a bit of a penny-pincher with your family. Those karmic seeds are waiting to sprout in different forms in future lifetimes.

Prarabdha Karma (The Active Balance)

This is the karma you're currently experiencing. It's the portion of your past actions that have ripened and are influencing your present life. Essentially, it's the hand you've been dealt.

Example: Ever wondered why some people are born into wealth while others struggle? Or why some seem naturally gifted while others work tirelessly? That's Prarabdha karma at work. It's like a Netflix series you started watching in a past life but now have to finish—even if it's a drama you're not thrilled about.

Agami/Kriyamana Karma (The Future Deposit)

This is the karma you're generating in the present. Your actions today will influence your tomorrow, just like your workout routine (or lack thereof) shapes your health. This is where free will comes into play, giving you the power to make conscious choices.

Example: Deciding to help a stranger or choosing to binge-watch shows all weekend—both create karma. The former adds to your good karma, while the latter... well, let's just say it contributes to your couch's wear and tear karma.

3. Other Dimensions of Karma

Beyond the basic types, karma has layers and nuances that make it even more fascinating. Let's delve into some additional aspects:

Nishkama Karma (Selfless Action)

This is karma performed without attachment to the results. Think of it as the gold standard of actions. The Bhagavad Gita emphasizes this concept, urging us to focus on our duties without worrying about outcomes.

Example: Volunteering at a shelter without expecting recognition is Nishkama karma. It's like giving a gift without checking if the recipient likes it or posts about it on social media.

Karma Yoga (The Path of Action)

One of the four primary paths to spiritual liberation in Hinduism, Karma Yoga is all about using your daily work as a means to grow spiritually. Whether you're a teacher, artist, or software developer, every action can become a form of worship if done with mindfulness.

Example: A chef cooking with love and care creates not just delicious meals but also positive energy. Compare this to someone microwaving leftovers while grumbling—big difference in karmic vibes!

Collective Karma

While we're busy managing our individual karma, there's also the concept of collective karma. This refers to the shared karma of groups, communities, or even nations.

Example: Environmental degradation is a product of humanity's collective karma. On the flip side, collective efforts like global charity initiatives also generate positive karma.

4. Misconceptions About Karma

Let's address some common myths about karma:

- **Myth 1: Karma is Punishment.** No, karma isn't out to get you. It's a neutral law, like gravity. If you trip and fall, it's not gravity's fault. Similarly, karma reflects your actions without bias.

- **Myth 2: Karma Acts Immediately.** While some effects show up quickly (spilling coffee after mocking someone's outfit), many take time. Patience, grasshopper.
- **Myth 3: Karma Is Fatalistic.** Karma doesn't mean you're doomed. It offers you choices and opportunities to shape your future.

5. Practical Application of Foundational Concepts

How can we integrate these karmic principles into daily life? Here are some tips:

1. **Mindful Actions:** Before acting, ask yourself, "What's my intention?" Even a small shift in mindset can create a ripple effect of positivity.
2. **Accountability:** Stop blaming Mercury retrograde for your troubles. Reflect on your choices and learn from them.
3. **Gratitude:** Recognize the role of Prarabdha karma in your life. Gratitude can help you navigate challenges with grace.

4. **Service:** Engage in Nishkama karma. Volunteer, help a neighbor, or simply smile at a stranger.

This foundational understanding of karma isn't just a philosophical exercise. It's a toolkit for navigating life with wisdom, humor, and a sense of purpose. After all, if karma's always watching, why not give it a good show?

Chapter 2

Philosophical Dimensions of Karma

The foundational understanding of karma introduces us to its mechanics, but to truly grasp its depth, we must explore its philosophical dimensions. These aspects reveal the profound wisdom behind karma and its relevance in our daily lives. Let's embark on this exploration by delving into the laws, intentions, and choices that govern karma.

---

1. The Law of Cause and Effect

At the heart of karma lies the universal law of cause and effect: every action produces a corresponding reaction. This principle isn't just confined to Hindu philosophy; it resonates with Newton's third law in physics and even the butterfly effect in chaos theory. The difference? Karma operates on both physical and metaphysical planes.

Understanding the Ripple Effect

Imagine dropping a pebble into a calm pond. The ripples spread outward, touching every corner.

Similarly, your actions create ripples that affect not just your life but also the lives of others.

Example: A kind word to a colleague might brighten their day, prompting them to pass on the kindness to someone else. Conversely, snapping at a cashier could ruin their day and create a chain of negativity. Your actions have consequences far beyond what you can see.

Karma in the Modern World

Consider social media. A single tweet can go viral, influencing opinions, sparking debates, or inspiring movements. Whether it's uplifting or divisive depends on the intent and content behind the action. It's karma in real-time.

2. Intention vs. Action

If karma were a courtroom, intention would be the star witness. Actions matter, but the motivations behind them are equally crucial. The Bhagavad Gita emphasizes that selfless actions, performed without attachment to the outcome, generate positive karma.

The Weight of Intention

Imagine two people donating to charity. One gives to gain publicity, while the other gives out of genuine compassion. The outward action is the same, but the karmic outcomes differ vastly because of their intentions.

Practical Example: Let's say you help a friend move to a new house. If your motivation is to bond and support them, it creates positive energy. If you're doing it begrudgingly, hoping for a favor in return, the karma isn't as uplifting.

The Gray Areas

Sometimes, intentions and outcomes don't align. For instance, you might give unsolicited advice with good intentions, but it's received poorly. While your intention was positive, the action created a less-than-desirable ripple. This is why mindfulness in both thought and action is essential.

3. The Role of Free Will and Destiny

One of the most debated aspects of karma is the interplay between free will and destiny. Are we merely puppets of our past karma, or do we have the power to change our fate? The answer lies in the balance between the two.

Destiny: The Hand You're Dealt

Prarabdha karma, as we discussed earlier, is like the cards you've been dealt in this lifetime. Your birthplace, family, and inherent talents are part of this karmic package. But destiny isn't a life sentence; it's more like a syllabus for your spiritual growth.

Example: You might be born with a natural inclination for music (destiny), but whether you practice and excel depends on your free will.

Free Will: The Choices You Make

Kriyamana karma represents the choices you're making right now. These actions can either reinforce your current trajectory or steer you toward a new path.

Practical Scenario: Imagine being stuck in traffic (a result of Prarabdha karma). You have two choices: curse your luck and get frustrated or use the time to listen to an audiobook or reflect. Your reaction shapes your immediate karma.

The Dynamic Relationship

Think of free will and destiny as a dance. Destiny sets the rhythm, but your choices determine the choreography. By exercising free will wisely, you can even mitigate the effects of certain karmic debts.

4. Karma and Dharma: A Symbiotic Relationship

Karma doesn't operate in isolation; it intertwines with **dharma** (righteous duty). Fulfilling your dharma aligns your actions with the universal order, creating harmony and reducing karmic burdens.

Understanding Dharma

Dharma isn't a rigid rulebook; it's your ethical compass. For a teacher, dharma might mean imparting knowledge sincerely. For a parent, it's nurturing their child with love and care.

Example: Arjuna in the Mahabharata struggled with his dharma as a warrior. Krishna's counsel in the Bhagavad Gita reminds him that performing his duty selflessly, without attachment to the results, is the essence of karma yoga.

Modern-Day Dharma

In today's world, your dharma could range from doing your job ethically to standing up for social justice. By aligning your actions with your higher purpose, you generate positive karma.

5. Karma and Interconnectedness

Karma isn't just about individual actions; it's a reminder of our interconnectedness. Your actions don't exist in a vacuum; they impact others and, in turn, circle back to you.

Collective Karma

As members of a family, community, or nation, we share collective karma. Environmental issues, for instance, are the result of humanity's collective actions over centuries. Similarly, global efforts to combat climate change represent positive collective karma.

Example: Recycling might seem like a small act, but when millions participate, the collective impact can be transformative.

Practical Wisdom

Recognizing interconnectedness encourages empathy. Before acting, consider how your choices affect others. Something as simple as treating service staff kindly contributes to a ripple of positivity.

6. The Karmic Feedback Loop

Karma operates in cycles, creating a feedback loop that teaches us lessons and encourages growth. The key is to recognize patterns and break unhelpful cycles.

Identifying Patterns

Do you often find yourself in similar situations—toxic relationships, financial struggles, or recurring conflicts? These patterns might indicate unresolved karmic lessons.

Example: If you frequently clash with authoritative figures, it might reflect an unresolved issue with accepting guidance or boundaries. Recognizing this allows you to approach such situations with a fresh perspective.

Breaking the Cycle

To break negative karmic patterns:

1. Reflect on past actions and their consequences.
2. Practice forgiveness—both for yourself and others.
3. Consciously choose actions that align with your higher self.

7. The Humor in Karma

Let's face it, karma has a sense of humor. Ever mocked someone for tripping, only to stumble moments later? It's the universe's playful reminder to stay humble.

Everyday Humor

- Criticizing someone's driving only to realize your own parking skills need work? Classic karmic irony.
- Posting a perfect vacation photo, then getting sunburned the next day? Karma's keeping it real.

Embracing karma's lighthearted moments helps us navigate life with grace and resilience.

Conclusion

The philosophical dimensions of karma reveal its profound complexity and practicality. From understanding the law of cause and effect to navigating the interplay of free will and destiny, these insights empower us to live more consciously. By aligning our actions with dharma, recognizing interconnectedness, and embracing the karmic feedback loop, we can create a life filled with purpose, growth, and a touch of humor. After all, karma isn't just about what happens to you; it's about who you become in the process. Write Notes Here:

Chapter 3:

Karma and Dharma

While karma is the universal law of cause and effect, **dharma** serves as the compass guiding those actions. The interplay between these two forces shapes the moral and ethical fabric of our lives. In this chapter, we will delve into their relationship, illustrated through examples from Hindu mythology, and explore how understanding dharma enriches our comprehension of karma.

---

1. Relationship Between Karma and Dharma

The relationship between karma and dharma can be likened to the roots and soil of a tree. Dharma, often translated as "duty," "righteousness," or "moral law," provides the ethical context within which karma operates. While karma is the action, dharma dictates the intention and alignment of that action with cosmic principles.

Dharma as the Foundation of Right Action

The **Bhagavad Gita** emphasizes that performing one's dharma, regardless of its challenges, is the highest form of karma. For example, Arjuna's dharma as a Kshatriya (warrior) compels him to fight in the Kurukshetra war, even though it involves battling his own relatives. Krishna reminds him that shirking his duty out of personal attachment would generate negative karma.

The Conflict Between Karma and Dharma

At times, dharma is not straightforward. Life's complexities can create situations where one must choose between competing dharmas. This is where wisdom, discernment, and the guidance of spiritual teachings become crucial.

Example: Imagine a doctor faced with the dilemma of prioritizing one critically ill patient over another due to resource constraints. The karma of their decision will depend on how closely it aligns with their dharma of saving lives impartially.

2. Examples From Hindu Mythology

Hindu mythology is rich with stories that illustrate the intricate dance between karma and dharma. Let's explore two prominent epics, the **Ramayana** and the **Mahabharata**, to see these principles in action.

The Ramayana: Rama's Adherence to Dharma

Lord Rama's life is a textbook example of upholding dharma despite personal sacrifices.

- **Exile and the Law of Dharma:** When Queen Kaikeyi demands that King Dasharatha exile Rama and crown her son Bharata instead, Rama unhesitatingly accepts the decision. His dharma as a son is to honor his father's word, even at the cost of his rightful throne. By choosing dharma over personal ambition, Rama sets a high standard for righteous action.
- **The Golden Deer Incident:** In the forest, Sita asks Rama to capture a golden deer. Despite knowing it might be an illusion, Rama fulfills her wish, as his dharma as a husband is to honor his wife's desires. This act, however, sets off a chain of events leading to

Sita's abduction by Ravana, illustrating how even dharmic actions can have complex karmic repercussions.

The Mahabharata: Krishna's Pragmatic Dharma

If Rama represents idealism, Krishna embodies pragmatism. His actions often blur the lines between dharma and adharma (unrighteousness) to achieve a greater good.

- **The Bhagavad Gita:** Krishna's counsel to Arjuna during the Kurukshetra war is a masterclass in balancing karma and dharma. He advises Arjuna to rise above his emotional turmoil and perform his dharma as a warrior, emphasizing that inaction is also a form of karma with its own consequences.
- **Karma in the Dice Game:** The infamous dice game where Yudhishthira loses his kingdom and Draupadi is humiliated raises questions about dharma. While Yudhishthira's adherence to the rules of the game aligns with his dharma as a king, his blind trust in Shakuni's intentions results in negative karma for everyone involved.

3. Dharma's Role in Shaping Karma

Dharma acts as the moral and ethical filter through which karma is processed. It prevents actions driven by selfishness, greed, or ignorance, ensuring that karma contributes to harmony rather than chaos.

Nishkama Dharma: Selfless Duty

The **Bhagavad Gita** promotes the idea of **nishkama dharma** — performing one's duty without attachment to the results. This mindset aligns karma with dharma, ensuring actions are driven by purity of intent rather than personal gain.

Example: A teacher imparting knowledge selflessly, without expecting accolades or material rewards, generates positive karma aligned with their dharma.

Adharma and Its Consequences

When actions deviate from dharma, they lead to adharma, or unrighteousness, which results in negative karma.

Example: Ravana's abduction of Sita violates dharma on multiple levels, from disrespecting a woman's autonomy to breaking the ethical codes of hospitality and kingship. His actions not only lead to his downfall but also bring suffering to his entire kingdom.

4. Modern Interpretations of Karma and Dharma

In today's context, understanding karma and dharma helps us navigate ethical dilemmas in personal and professional life.

Workplace Ethics

- **Karma Without Dharma:** A salesperson achieving targets through manipulation may enjoy short-term success but will likely face karmic repercussions, such as losing trust or tarnishing their reputation.

- **Karma Aligned With Dharma:** On the other hand, a leader prioritizing transparency and fairness generates trust and long-term goodwill, creating positive karma for themselves and their organization.

Relationships

- **Balancing Personal and Social Dharma:** Consider a person torn between caring for aging parents and pursuing a demanding career abroad. Aligning karma with dharma involves honest communication, setting boundaries, and finding ways to fulfill both responsibilities to the best of their ability.

5. Practical Lessons From Karma and Dharma

1. **Discernment:** Before acting, ask yourself if your actions align with your personal and social dharma.
2. **Reflection:** Regularly evaluate the impact of your actions on yourself and others. Are they creating harmony or conflict?
3. **Adaptability:** Recognize that dharma is dynamic. What's righteous in one situation may not be so in another. Stay open to recalibrating your actions.

4. **Service:** Engage in actions that benefit others, such as volunteering, mentoring, or simply being kind. These acts align karma with dharma and enrich your life.

Karma and dharma are not abstract concepts but practical tools for leading a balanced and purposeful life. By understanding their relationship, we can make more informed choices, navigate challenges with grace, and contribute to a more harmonious world.

Chapter 4:

Practical Implications of Karma

Karma, as a concept, is deeply philosophical, but its value truly unfolds when applied to everyday life. Understanding how karma influences our actions, decisions, and relationships allows us to lead a more mindful and harmonious existence. In this chapter, we will explore karma's practical dimensions, covering its role in daily life, ethical considerations, and ways to navigate and overcome past karma.

---

1. Karma in Everyday Life

The principle of karma is not confined to esoteric spiritual practices or the annals of ancient philosophy. It's woven into the fabric of our everyday experiences, influencing how we interact with others, make decisions, and shape our lives.

Actions and Reactions: The Domino Effect

Every action we take sets off a chain reaction, like a series of dominoes falling. The way we speak to a colleague, treat a stranger, or respond to a challenge creates ripples that affect not just others but also ourselves.

Example: Imagine you're at a coffee shop. The barista gets your order wrong, and you respond angrily. Your negative energy might ruin their day, leading them to make more mistakes, which affects other customers. Alternatively, responding with kindness could uplift their mood, creating a positive ripple effect.

Daily Decisions

Karma reminds us that small, everyday decisions matter. Choosing to recycle, help a neighbor, or practice patience during a traffic jam are all karmic acts that contribute to the larger narrative of our lives.

Tip: Begin each day with the intention of creating positive karma. A simple affirmation like, "May my actions bring joy and harmony," can set the tone for mindful living.

2. Ethical and Moral Dimensions

Karma is deeply intertwined with ethics and morality, acting as an inner compass that guides our actions. It prompts us to consider not just what we do but why and how we do it.

The Ethics of Intention

The moral weight of an action is heavily influenced by the intention behind it. An act performed with pure intent generates positive karma, even if the outcome is not as expected.

Example: Donating to charity with genuine compassion, even if the funds are mismanaged by the organization, creates good karma. Conversely, giving solely for public recognition dilutes the karmic value of the act.

Navigating Moral Dilemmas

Life often presents situations where the "right" choice isn't immediately clear. In such cases, karma encourages us to act with integrity and consider the broader implications of our decisions.

Example: A business owner facing financial difficulties might be tempted to cut corners or exploit employees. Acting ethically, even at personal cost, aligns their karma with dharma and fosters long-term success.

The Golden Rule of Karma

The ethical essence of karma aligns with the principle of reciprocity: "Treat others as you wish to be treated." This golden rule serves as a universal guide for ethical living, transcending cultural and religious boundaries.

3. Overcoming Past Karma Through Self-Awareness

While we cannot escape the consequences of past actions, karma offers pathways to mitigate their impact and chart a more positive course for the future.

Acknowledgment and Accountability

The first step in overcoming past karma is to acknowledge it without denial or self-pity. Accepting responsibility for past actions empowers us to make amends and learn from our mistakes.

Example: If strained relationships are a recurring theme in your life, reflect on whether past actions—such as neglect or harsh words—might have contributed. Taking steps to apologize and rebuild trust can help dissolve negative karma.

Practicing Mindfulness

Mindfulness—the art of being fully present—is a powerful tool for breaking karmic cycles. By observing our thoughts and actions without judgment, we can identify patterns that perpetuate negative karma.

Exercise: Spend five minutes each day reflecting on your actions. Ask yourself, "Did I act with kindness and integrity today?" This simple practice can lead to profound self-awareness.

Cultivating Positive Karma

Engage in acts of kindness, generosity, and compassion to offset past karma. While the goal isn't to "neutralize" karma like a ledger, these actions create a reservoir of positive energy that uplifts you and those around you.

Example: Volunteering at a local shelter or mentoring someone in need not only benefits others but also enriches your own karmic journey.

4. The Role of Forgiveness in Karma

Forgiveness, both of oneself and others, is a transformative practice that helps dissolve negative karmic imprints.

Self-Forgiveness

Often, we are our harshest critics. Holding onto guilt or regret from past actions can create a cycle of self-punishment that perpetuates negative karma.

Exercise: Write a letter to yourself, acknowledging past mistakes and expressing forgiveness. Let this act serve as a symbolic release of self-blame.

Forgiving Others

Forgiving someone who has wronged you doesn't absolve their actions but frees you from the burden of resentment.

Example: A woman who forgives her estranged father for abandoning the family may find herself liberated from years of bitterness, allowing her to build healthier relationships.

5. Karma in Relationships

Relationships are fertile ground for karmic dynamics, offering opportunities for growth, healing, and transformation.

Karmic Patterns

Recurring themes in relationships often indicate unresolved karmic lessons. Recognizing these patterns is the first step toward breaking them.

Example: A person repeatedly attracting controlling partners might need to address their own issues with self-worth and boundaries.

The Power of Reciprocity

Healthy relationships thrive on mutual respect and effort. Investing time, energy, and love in your relationships generates positive karma and strengthens bonds.

Tip: Practice active listening and express gratitude in your interactions. These simple acts create a foundation of trust and positivity.

6. The Karmic Cycle and Spiritual Growth

Karma isn't just about balancing the scales; it's a vehicle for spiritual evolution. Every challenge, setback, and triumph is an opportunity to grow in wisdom and compassion.

Turning Challenges Into Lessons

Instead of viewing difficulties as punishments, see them as opportunities to learn and grow. This perspective shifts your relationship with karma from one of victimhood to empowerment.

Example: Losing a job might initially seem like a negative karmic event, but it could lead to self-discovery, new opportunities, and a more fulfilling career.

Practicing Detachment

Detachment—not to be confused with indifference—is the practice of letting go of excessive attachment to outcomes. It allows us to act with sincerity while remaining open to whatever results.

Exercise: Before making a significant decision, take a moment to breathe deeply and remind yourself, "I will do my best and accept the outcome."

7. Practical Steps for Karmic Alignment

To integrate the principles of karma into your life, consider these actionable steps:

1. **Set Intentions:** Begin each day with a clear intention to act with kindness and integrity.
2. **Reflect Regularly:** Dedicate time to reflect on your actions and their impact on others.
3. **Serve Others:** Engage in selfless acts of service, from volunteering to simple gestures of kindness.

4. **Seek Knowledge:** Study spiritual teachings and philosophies to deepen your understanding of karma.

5. **Embrace Gratitude:** Cultivate an attitude of gratitude for both the blessings and lessons in your life.

Conclusion

Understanding karma's practical implications transforms it from an abstract concept into a powerful tool for personal and spiritual growth. By aligning our actions with ethical principles, cultivating self-awareness, and embracing life's challenges as opportunities, we can navigate the karmic landscape with grace and purpose. After all, as the saying goes, "What you plant now, you will harvest later." Let's ensure we're planting seeds of kindness, integrity, and love.

Chapter 5:

Comparative Study of Karma

Karma, as a concept, transcends the boundaries of Hindu philosophy and finds resonance in several other spiritual and religious traditions. While the nuances may differ, the core idea of actions and their consequences remains central. In this chapter, we explore karma in Buddhism, Jainism, Sikhism, and other traditions, comparing similarities and differences to enrich our understanding.

---

1. Karma in Other Traditions

Buddhism

In Buddhism, karma (or "kamma" in Pali) is a fundamental tenet closely tied to the cycle of birth, death, and rebirth ('samsara'). It emphasizes intentionality ('cetana') as the driving force behind karma, highlighting that it's not just what you do but why and how you do it that matters. The Buddha taught that actions rooted in greed, hatred, or delusion result in suffering, while those inspired by generosity, love, and wisdom lead to positive outcomes.

Key Points:

- **Intentionality is Paramount:** For example, accidentally stepping on an ant doesn't generate negative karma, but intentionally harming it does.
- **Noble Eightfold Path:** Right action, speech, and livelihood are crucial to accumulating good karma and progressing toward Nirvana.
- **Karmic Seeds:** Buddhism often uses the metaphor of seeds to describe karma. Actions plant seeds that may ripen in this life or future ones, influencing the nature of existence.

Jainism

Jainism takes a more literal and detailed approach to karma. It describes karma as a form of fine matter that binds to the soul due to passions like anger, pride, deceit, and greed. Liberation ('moksha') is only possible when one purges these karmic particles through ascetic practices and self-discipline.

Key Points:

- **Karma as Physical Substance:** Karma is seen as a material entity that attaches to the soul, weighing it down and perpetuating the cycle of rebirth.
- **Ahimsa (Non-violence):** Extreme non-violence is practiced to avoid generating harmful karma. Even accidentally harming a living being can attract negative karma.
- **Self-Purification:** Practices like fasting, meditation, and self-restraint help burn accumulated karma.

Sikhism

In Sikhism, karma is acknowledged but placed within the broader framework of divine grace ('Nadar'). While actions do have consequences, ultimate liberation depends on God's will. This perspective balances personal responsibility with surrender to divine wisdom.

Key Points:

- **Karma and Grace:** Good deeds (like serving others) create positive karma, but spiritual liberation ('mukti') comes from divine mercy.

- **Egolessness:** Ego ('haumai') is considered the root cause of karma, and overcoming it through devotion and humility is essential.
- **Equality and Service:** The emphasis on serving humanity reflects the Sikh belief in collective karma and shared responsibility.

Other Traditions

- **Taoism:** While karma isn't explicitly discussed, Taoist philosophy embraces the idea of harmony and balance, akin to the karmic principle of cause and effect.
- **Western Philosophy:** Concepts like "what you sow, so shall you reap" in Christian teachings echo karmic ideas, though often framed within divine judgment rather than cyclical rebirth.

2. Differences and Similarities

Similarities Across Traditions

1. **Cause and Effect:** The core principle of actions leading to consequences is universal.

2. **Ethical Living:** All traditions emphasize ethical conduct, compassion, and self-awareness as pathways to positive outcomes.

3. **Liberation as a Goal:** Whether it's Nirvana, Moksha, or Mukti, transcending the cycle of cause and effect is a shared aspiration.

Differences Across Traditions

1. **Nature of Karma:** Jainism's literal interpretation as a physical substance differs from Buddhism's focus on intention and Sikhism's integration of divine grace.

2. **Role of Divine Intervention:** Hinduism and Sikhism incorporate the role of divinity, while Jainism and Buddhism are more self-reliant systems.

3. **Practical Application:** Jainism's extreme practices (like wearing masks to avoid harming microorganisms) contrast with Sikhism's more accessible approach of community service and devotion.

3. Unique Interpretations and Practices

Collective Karma

Several traditions recognize the idea of collective karma, where communities or nations experience shared outcomes based on collective actions.

Example: Environmental crises can be viewed as humanity's collective karma, emphasizing the need for global responsibility and cooperation.

Instant Karma

Pop culture often highlights the idea of instant karma, where actions yield immediate consequences. While this isn't always how karma operates in spiritual traditions, it serves as a reminder of the interconnectedness of actions and results.

Example: Cutting someone off in traffic and getting stuck in a jam shortly after feels like an amusing nod to karmic justice!

Reincarnation and Karma

The idea that karma carries over into future lives is central to Hinduism, Buddhism, and Jainism but is less emphasized in Sikhism and absent in Western traditions. This difference influences practices and priorities in each system.

4. Practical Takeaways from the Comparative Study

- **Intentional Living:** Regardless of tradition, living with awareness and good intentions is universally valued.
- **Balance Responsibility and Grace:** Combining personal effort with humility and acceptance can provide a balanced approach to karma.
- **Focus on the Present:** While understanding past karma is helpful, all traditions stress the importance of present actions in shaping the future.

Conclusion

Studying karma across traditions reveals both its universal relevance and the richness of its interpretations. Each system offers unique insights, from Buddhism's emphasis on intention to Jainism's rigorous discipline and Sikhism's blend of karma and divine grace. By exploring these perspectives, we can deepen our understanding and apply the principles of karma more effectively in our lives, appreciating the diverse ways humanity seeks to unravel the mysteries of existence.

Chapter 6:

Conclusion

After journeying through the intricate landscapes of karma, exploring its origins, philosophical dimensions, and practical implications, we arrive at the final chapter of our exploration. This chapter ties together the wisdom gleaned, offering reflections, practical guidance, and an invitation to embrace karma as a guiding force for conscious living.

---

1. Summarizing Insights

Karma, as we've seen, is more than a mystical doctrine; it's a profound framework that connects actions, intentions, and consequences. Through its lens, life becomes an intricate tapestry where every thread matters.

- **Origins and Foundations:** From the Vedic hymns to the Upanishads, karma evolved from ritualistic actions to a deeply personal and spiritual principle.

- **Philosophical Dimensions:** The interplay of cause and effect, the balance between free will and destiny, and the role of intention in shaping outcomes demonstrate karma's depth.

- **Interconnected Concepts:** The harmony between karma and dharma, as exemplified in the Ramayana and Mahabharata, highlights the importance of aligning actions with righteousness.

- **Comparative Perspectives:** Across Buddhism, Jainism, Sikhism, and other traditions, karma emerges as a universal principle, interpreted uniquely but emphasizing personal accountability.

Through these layers, karma reveals itself not as a deterministic cage but as a tool for self-empowerment and growth.

Anecdote:

In the Mahabharata, we see Yudhishthira's unwavering commitment to dharma, even when confronted with immense adversity. His actions, guided by righteousness, ultimately earned him a place in heaven, underscoring the principle that karma, aligned with dharma, leads to ultimate liberation.

2. Practical Takeaways

Understanding karma isn't just an intellectual exercise; it's a guide for living a balanced and meaningful life. Here are some actionable insights:

Mindfulness in Actions

Every choice we make, no matter how small, contributes to the karmic ledger. Practicing mindfulness helps ensure our actions align with our values.

Example: Before reacting in anger, pause and reflect on the impact. A harsh word can create lasting scars, while a kind word can uplift someone's spirit.

Intention Matters

Actions driven by pure intentions hold greater karmic value. Nishkama karma, or selfless action, teaches us to focus on the deed rather than the reward.

Example: A mother's unconditional love for her child is the epitome of selfless action. She nurtures without expecting returns, creating positive energy.

Taking Accountability

Karma encourages us to own our actions and their consequences. Blaming others or circumstances only delays personal growth.

Example: A student who fails an exam has two choices—blame the teacher or assess their preparation. The latter leads to learning and improvement.

Cultivating Good Karma

Simple acts of kindness can ripple outwards, creating a cycle of positivity.

Example: Helping a struggling colleague or donating anonymously generates goodwill and uplifts the collective karmic balance.

Overcoming Past Karma

Self-awareness and deliberate effort can mitigate the effects of negative karma.

Example: Valmiki, who transformed from a bandit to a sage, illustrates the power of repentance and conscious living in altering one's karmic trajectory.

3. Call to Introspection and Conscious Living

Karma invites us to reflect deeply on our lives, fostering a sense of responsibility and intentionality. It's a reminder that life isn't happening to us; it's responding to us.

The Ripple Effect

Imagine a pond. A single pebble creates ripples that touch every corner. Similarly, our actions influence not just our lives but also those around us.

Aligning with Dharma

Living in alignment with one's dharma amplifies the positive impact of karma. Dharma varies for everyone—it could mean being a dedicated parent, a compassionate leader, or a diligent student.

Story: In the Ramayana, Hanuman's unwavering devotion to Rama exemplifies living in accordance with dharma. His selfless service, driven by love and purpose, made him a timeless symbol of devotion and righteousness.

Releasing Attachments

Attachment to outcomes often leads to disappointment. The Bhagavad Gita advises focusing on the action, not the result. This detachment fosters peace and equanimity.

Example: A gardener plants seeds without obsessing over each one's growth. They trust the process, knowing they've done their part.

4. Embracing Karma in Modern Times

In today's fast-paced world, the principle of karma is more relevant than ever. It encourages mindfulness in an era of distractions, accountability in a culture of blame, and compassion in a time of division.

Karma in Relationships

Treating others with kindness and respect fosters stronger bonds and reduces conflict.

Example: Apologizing sincerely when wrong builds trust and mends relationships, creating positive karmic energy.

Karma in Career

Integrity and effort in professional life lead to long-term success. Cutting corners might yield quick gains but creates negative karma.

Example: An employee who mentors juniors and shares credit earns goodwill, which often translates into career growth.

Karma and Mental Health

Letting go of guilt and embracing forgiveness can lighten the karmic load and enhance well-being.

Story: A monk once carried a grudge against a fellow disciple. Realizing the weight of his resentment, he forgave and experienced immediate inner peace.

5. The Eternal Journey

Karma reminds us that life is an ongoing journey of learning and evolving. Each moment offers a chance to reset, to act with wisdom, and to contribute positively to the world.

Parable:

A seeker once asked a sage, "When will I be free of karma?" The sage replied, "When you realize you are both the weaver and the thread." This profound insight underscores that we shape our destinies through our actions and intentions.

Inspiration from Nature

Nature operates on karmic principles. A tree provides shade and fruit selflessly, embodying the spirit of Nishkama karma. Observing such examples can inspire us to act with grace and generosity.

6. Final Reflection

As we close this exploration, remember that karma isn't a distant, esoteric concept. It's a dynamic force, present in every thought, word, and deed. By understanding and embracing its principles, we not only enrich our own lives but also contribute to a harmonious world.

Invitation: Take a moment today to reflect on your actions. Are they aligned with your values? Do they uplift others? In this quiet introspection lies the seed of transformation.

Closing Thought: Life, with its joys and challenges, is a canvas. Karma is the brush, and your actions are the strokes. Paint wisely, and you'll create a masterpiece worth cherishing.

Final Chapter:

Insights from Adi Shankaracharya and Swami Vivekananda on Karma

As we conclude this exploration of karma, it is fitting to delve into the profound insights offered by two towering figures in Indian philosophy—Adi Shankaracharya and Swami Vivekananda. Their perspectives not only illuminate the nuanced dimensions of karma but also provide practical guidance for navigating its complexities. Through their teachings, we find a bridge between ancient wisdom and contemporary understanding, underscoring the timeless relevance of karma.

---

1. Adi Shankaracharya: The Advaitic Perspective

Adi Shankaracharya, the proponent of Advaita Vedanta, viewed karma through the lens of non-dualism. His teachings emphasize the ultimate reality, **Brahman**, and the role of karma in the journey toward liberation (moksha).

Karma as a Tool, Not the Goal

Shankaracharya argued that while karma governs the empirical world, it is not the ultimate truth. In his commentary on the Brahmasutras, he explained that karma binds individuals to the cycle of birth and rebirth (samsara). However, this bondage is not permanent. Self-realization—the recognition of one's identity with Brahman—is the ultimate goal, transcending the effects of karma.

- **Example:** Shankaracharya's analogy of the pot and clay is enlightening. Just as a pot made of clay eventually returns to its original form, an individual's true essence remains untouched by karma, even as actions create ripples in the material world.

Jnana vs. Karma

Shankaracharya emphasized the supremacy of **jnana (knowledge)** over karma. He believed that while good deeds are essential for purifying the mind, they cannot directly lead to liberation. Only knowledge of the self can dissolve ignorance (avidya), which is the root cause of karma.

- **Story from Shankaracharya's Life:** One of the most famous anecdotes illustrating his philosophy involves a disciple who questioned the role of karma. Shankaracharya explained: *"Karma can light the lamp of self-purification, but only the flame of knowledge can dispel the darkness of ignorance."*

Relevance in Modern Life

For those grappling with the weight of actions and their consequences, Shankaracharya's teachings offer solace. He reminds us that while karma is inevitable, it does not define our essence. Meditation, self-inquiry, and detachment can help us rise above its grip.

2. Swami Vivekananda: The Practical Visionary

Swami Vivekananda brought a pragmatic approach to the theory of karma, blending ancient wisdom with modern sensibilities. He emphasized action (karma yoga) as a means of spiritual growth and societal transformation.

Karma Yoga: The Path of Selfless Action

Vivekananda's interpretation of karma yoga resonates with the Bhagavad Gita's call to act without attachment. He believed that selfless action, performed with the welfare of others in mind, is the highest form of worship.

- **Example:** In one of his lectures, Vivekananda narrated the story of a farmer who toiled diligently but shared his harvest generously. The farmer's selfless actions not only brought him peace but also uplifted his community.

The Interplay of Free Will and Destiny

Vivekananda's view on free will and destiny is particularly striking. He acknowledged the influence of past karma but insisted that humans are not powerless. By exercising free will, individuals can shape their future.

- **Example:** He often cited the analogy of a cow tethered to a post. The cow's movement is limited by the length of the rope (destiny), but within that range, it has freedom (free will).

Our actions today determine whether the rope tightens or loosens tomorrow.

Breaking the Chains of Karma

Vivekananda believed that karma could be transformed through conscious effort. He urged people to:

1. **Cultivate Awareness:** Understand the motives behind actions.
2. **Serve Others:** Engage in acts of kindness to neutralize negative karma.
3. **Embrace Detachment:** Perform duties without expecting rewards.

- **Example:** In his own life, Vivekananda's relentless efforts to uplift the poor and educate the masses exemplified karma yoga. He lived what he preached, inspiring millions to follow his path.

3. The Relativeness of Karma: A Unified Perspective

Both Shankaracharya and Vivekananda offer complementary views on the relativeness of karma. While Shankaracharya focuses on transcending karma through knowledge, Vivekananda emphasizes transforming karma through action. Together, they present a holistic framework for understanding and engaging with karma.

Karma as a Balancing Act

Karma is inherently relative, shaped by intention, context, and perspective. What may appear as a burden to one person might be an opportunity for growth to another. This relativeness is beautifully illustrated in mythology:

- **Example from the Ramayana:** When Rama accepted exile, his actions seemed like a consequence of karma. Yet, his selflessness and adherence to dharma transformed the situation into an example of noble conduct. For Kaikeyi, the same event revealed how misguided intentions can lead to regret.

Intention vs. Outcome

The Mahabharata further illustrates the relativeness of karma. Arjuna's hesitation in the Kurukshetra war stemmed from his concern about the morality of killing. However, Krishna's counsel highlighted the importance of intention and duty. Actions aligned with dharma, even when difficult, contribute to positive karma.

4. Practical Insights for Modern Seekers

Balancing Knowledge and Action

Shankaracharya and Vivekananda remind us that life's challenges can be met through a balance of contemplation and action. While introspection reveals our true nature, purposeful action allows us to contribute meaningfully to the world.

Overcoming Karmic Debt

By combining self-awareness with selfless service, individuals can mitigate the effects of past karma. Practices such as meditation, charity, and ethical living create a positive ripple effect.

Empowering the Self

Both philosophers emphasize the power of self-effort. Shankaracharya's call to transcend and Vivekananda's urge to transform inspire us to take charge of our destinies.

5. Stories as Eternal Guides

The teachings of Shankaracharya and Vivekananda are filled with anecdotes that resonate across ages. Whether it is the potter's clay or the farmer's harvest, their metaphors and stories offer profound lessons for navigating the complexities of karma.

A Story of Redemption:

Vivekananda once narrated the tale of a thief who, after years of wrongdoing, turned to selfless service. By dedicating his life to helping others, he not only redeemed himself but also inspired a village to embrace collective good.

- The lesson: No matter how heavy one's karmic baggage, redemption is always possible through conscious effort.

A Story of Perspective:

Shankaracharya's story of the illusory snake and rope illustrates the relativeness of perception. What seems like a threat (the snake) often reveals itself as harmless (a rope) upon closer examination. Similarly, karma's challenges can transform into opportunities for growth with the right mindset.

6. Final Reflections

The teachings of Adi Shankaracharya and Swami Vivekananda illuminate the path of karma with depth and clarity. While their approaches differ, their messages converge on the idea that karma is not a chain binding us to fate but a tool for liberation and transformation. By embracing their wisdom, we can navigate life with greater awareness, purpose, and joy.

As we close this journey, let us carry forward their call to introspection and action. Whether through the lens of Advaita or the path of karma yoga, the choice is ours to transcend, transform, and thrive in the dance of karma.

References

1. **Bhagavad Gita**. (2000). *The Bhagavad Gita: A New Translation*. Eknath Easwaran. Nilgiri Press.

2. **Patanjali**. (2007). *Yoga Sutras of Patanjali*. Swami Sivananda. The Divine Life Society.

3. **Karma and Rebirth**. (1995). *The Law of Karma: A Philosophical Perspective*. Geshe Lhundub Sopa. Snow Lion Publications.

4. **Karma in Buddhist Philosophy**. (2010). *The Heart of the Buddha's Teaching*. Thich Nhat Hanh. Parallax Press.

5. **The Philosophy of Karma**. (1991). *A History of Indian Philosophy: Volume 1*. Surendranath Dasgupta. Cambridge University Press.

6. **The Theory of Karma: A Western Perspective**. (2003). *Karma: A Guide to Your Spiritual Journey*. Norman W. Ford. New World Library.

7. **Hindu Scriptures**. (1998). *The Upanishads*. Eknath Easwaran. Nilgiri Press.

8. **The Laws of Karma**. (2005). *The Law of Karma: What You Do Comes Back to You*. Robert A. Thurman. TarcherPerigee.

9. **The Bhagavad Gita and Its Message**. (2012). *Essays on the Bhagavad Gita*. Radhakrishnan, S. (Ed.). HarperCollins Publishers.

10. **The Concept of Karma**. (2000). *Karma and the Individual: The Influence of Past Actions on Life's Journey*. David S. W. Lee. Oxford University Press.

11. **Philosophical Interpretations of Karma**. (2015). *Karma, Destiny, and Free Will: A Philosophical Inquiry*. John W. Kirsch. Princeton University Press.

12. **The Science of Karma**. (2007). *Karma: The Mechanism of Reincarnation*. Michael Newton. Llewellyn Publications.

13. **The Role of Karma in Modern Psychology**. (2018). *Psychological Perspectives on Karma: Bridging the Gap Between East and West*. Arnold S. Naimark. Springer.

14. **Ancient Indian Thought on Karma**. (2000). *Indian Philosophy: An Introduction*. R. K. Dasgupta. Motilal Banarsidass Publishers.

15. **The Ramayana**. (2006). *The Ramayana: A Modern Translation*. R. K. Narayan. Penguin Classics.

16. **Scientific Views on Karma**. (2021). *The Neuroscience of Free Will and Karma*. David J. Chalmers. MIT Press.

17. **Jainism and Karma**. (1992). *Karma and the Doctrine of Jainism*. V. S. Jain. Jain Publications.

18. **The Karma of Success**. (2014). *The Secret to Achieving Your Dreams Through Karma*. Deepak Chopra. Hay House.

19. **Karma and Social Justice**. (2009). *Karma in Contemporary Society*. V. P. Verma. Sage Publications.

20. **The Path of Karma Yoga**. (2000). *Karma Yoga: The Path of Selfless Action*. Swami Vivekananda. Advaita Ashrama.

About the Author

Dr Pratul Sharma is an avid explorer of ancient wisdom and its relevance in modern life. With a deep-seated interest in spirituality, philosophy, and  human behavior, he has spent decades studying the intricate teachings of the Indian scriptures, including the Bhagavad Gita, Upanishads, and the Vedas. As a practitioner of Ayurveda and an experienced trainer in fields such as management and leadership, Dr Sharma brings a unique blend of ancient knowledge and contemporary perspectives to his work.

His extensive teaching experience has enabled him to distill complex concepts into practical insights, making timeless principles accessible to a modern audience.

Driven by a passion for understanding the deeper workings of life, Dr Pratul has written *Karma is Relative* to bridge the gap between traditional teachings and their application in today's world. His approach combines philosophical depth with practical wisdom, offering readers tools to navigate life with awareness and purpose.

In this book, he delves into karma as a universal law that transcends cultural and religious boundaries, providing a comprehensive exploration of its spiritual, philosophical, and scientific dimensions. Through his work, he seeks to inspire readers to live more consciously, understanding how every action contributes to the fabric of their destiny.

When he isn't writing or teaching, Dr Sharma enjoys exploring ancient texts, meditating, and sharing insights with those on the path of self-discovery.

Dr Sharma can be contacted through email on drpratuls@gmail.com

www.ingramcontent.com/pod-product-compliance
Lightning Source LLC
Chambersburg PA
CBHW020501160726
47991CB00007B/2767